KAMUTI

A new way in bonsai

KAMUTI

A new way in bonsai

by

WILLI E. BOLLMANN

faber and faber
LONDON · BOSTON

First published in 1974
This edition published in 1977
Reprinted in 1984 and 1989
by Faber and Faber Limited
3 Queen Square London WC1N 3AU
Printed in Great Britain by
Richard Clay Ltd, Bungay, Suffolk

BRITISH LIBRARY CATALOGUING IN PUBLICATION DATA

Bollmann, Willi E.
  Kamuti.
  1. Bonsai
  I. Title
  635.9'77   SB433.5

ISBN 0-571-11060-6

Contents

Contents

8

Illustrations

To D. L. DIEFENDERFER

ACKNOWLEDGEMENTS

I am extremely grateful to Mr. Sidney Harvey and to Mr. Martin Webb for their editorial assistance in the preparation of my text, and to Mrs. Denise Zwahlen who typed it for me. Photographs for plates 5 to 12 were kindly supplied by Mr. John Delé-Hoffmann.

Introduction

It was the tree which had been stunted by nature, the starving tree, struggling in poor soil conditions for many decades, that led to the production of the potted tree which is today known as Bonsai. Yes—nature was the very first to dwarf trees. The second in line was the nurseryman. Have a look round your local nursery, and you will find somewhere in a corner the 'left-overs', still in the same container in which they were planted years ago, and almost the same size as they were when first planted. Both nature and nurserymen have achieved dwarfing in the same way: through lack of nourishment. Incidentally, both have done it unintentionally.

In principle, the Japanese method of dwarfing, by supplying conditions similar to those produced by nature when they are imperfect, duplicates them in every detail. The container, by which the growth of the root system is limited, is the main agency used by the Japanese to dwarf a tree.

The container represents the small pocket of soil in between rocks, from observation of which the Japanese have learned of the dwarfing effect it has on trees of all kinds. Most of the old miniature trees that we admire today are trees originally dwarfed by nature, which were removed from their parent site, planted in containers, and then gradually perfected in appearance over a period of many years.

As a result of my experiments over the past seven years, I have found that the foliage and the branch formation of any tree can be dwarfed without limiting the roots at all. In other words, we can grow a miniature tree under perfectly normally healthy conditions. Based on the principles of what a tree needs and what it can give, it is possible to sculpture a perfect replica in small dimensions within three to five years.

It is for all those who really want to grow and create shapes in living trees that this book has been written. It describes a modern technique composed of hard and fast rules based on natural facts, this technique being a logical approach to the laws of nature and therefore valid under all climatic conditions.

BONSAI, ORIGIN AND DEVELOPMENT

For those who know nothing about Bonsai, the following notes provide a brief explanation.

All over the world where growing conditions are imperfect, nature produces stunted plants. Such plants grew in situ until someone happened to see an old specimen, a tree perhaps, living on the rocky slopes of the mountains. It might have been there for 30, 40 years, growing in a small pocket of soil contained by stones, giving the roots no chance to spread further. If the plant could stay alive and grow in such a small quantity of soil, then it should obviously be possible to transfer it to a container and keep it in the house, and so the first Bonsai may have been born, as a result of doing that very thing. We do not know when the art was actually started, but the Japanese have written about Bonsai, and have pictorial records dating back to about A.D. 1200. The raising of Bonsai from a seed or cutting, however, is comparatively recent and was begun about 200 years ago.

The word 'bonsai' means 'potted tree' or 'tree in a tray'. The emphasis is on the word TREE, but the plant in question need not necessarily be one—it can be a shrub, but its appearance has to be tree-like. This is what separates a Bonsai from all other plants in containers.

There is a popular misconception, not only in the Western world, but also within Japan, as to what exactly constitutes a Bonsai. Species of trees are kept in containers over long periods of time without developing any features which are tree-like at all. Sometimes they even flower and bear fruit, but in fact the appearance of these plants is more like that of the average seedling, consisting as they do, of a thick trunk with only two or three thin lateral shoots sticking out, often at ungainly angles (see p. 30, 'What makes a tree').

The ideal Bonsai is a tree the size of whose different parts are seen to be in exactly proportionate relation to each other. Trunk, branches, twigs and leaves are in complete harmony. A Bonsai can be either an exact replica of the species, or an artistic variation in shape.

In nature, the cause of dwarfed growth is lack of nourishment. Very sandy soil or a thin layer of soil over stones, and a shortage of rain, can lead to starvation of the plant, and hence to stunting. A tree collected from such a location has to be shaped over several decades to produce the image of a perfect miniature. Dwarfed trees in the open very seldom show even growth. Lack of nourishment results in imbalance and slows down the growing process.

It was only after the Second World War that the knowledge and appreciation of Bonsai spread within the Western world. In America, the Brooklyn Botanic Garden did a great deal to introduce Bonsai to a wider circle by inviting famous Japanese lecturers to the States to talk about the art, and by publishing books about their methods of cultivation.

Today, Bonsai societies are found in most parts of the world, and in America, Australia and South Africa Bonsai fanciers are trying their skill on their indigenous flora; in South Africa in particular the gigantic baobab (*Adansonia digitata*), famous for the extreme (30-ft.) thickness of its trunk, has been successfully dwarfed to miniatures of only 1 foot high.

It is appropriate to mention here that it is now possible to grow miniature trees to order. One can copy expressive examples of living trees, as well as trees in paintings, and sculpture them accordingly. Any desired size and shape can be achieved if the growing principles of this book are applied. It takes five years to establish a little tree, whereas with traditional techniques one has to wait thirty to fifty years to achieve a similar result.

THE LINK WITH ART

In all the arts we have constant development down the centuries, but it is in the last one that the range of expressions and techniques has widened most. The art of Bonsai, however, still stands where it stood centuries ago.

Suppose you wished to take up sculpture, woodwork or painting. The logical approach would be to become familiar with the materials and tools you would have to use, so that you could handle both to the greatest advantage. For sculpturing, you would need to know the way in which

a   b

c   d

Fig. 1   Sculpturing (formation of the tree by subtraction)   (a) the untouched block   (b) the image is inside, still hidden   (c) the image is gradually exposed by chipping away the surplus   (d) the final image

the different stones chip when worked on with various types of chisels. For woodwork, you would need to learn about the grain and fabric structure of your wood before you could carve and cut it successfully. If you take up painting, the wide range of effects and relations of colours must also be considered, besides the materials.

SCULPTURING

However, let us assume you know all this, and you begin to work. You will then have two possibilities: either you copy the masters of Bonsai, or you find your very own style of expression, bearing the following observations in mind.

When you sculpture in wood or stone, you start off with a solid, unformed block in front of you. This block contains in its volume the hidden shape of your imagination, which you intend to create by means of exposing. You chip, cut and chisel away the material until you have achieved and shown the shape you had in mind when you started (see figs. 1a–d).

With clay or plasticine, on the other hand, you would choose the modelling technique. First you would form your trunk, if it is a tree you wish to produce. Next, you would attach to the trunk some preformed branches, and finally add small twigs and their leaves (see figs. 2a–f).

This modelling technique is already closer to our sculpturing with living material, than is sculpturing itself, which uses an inert, lifeless mass. The only difference is that our material for the next step literally grows out of the previous one. One must, however, remember that nature has certain rules which we cannot override. For instance, new shoots or laterals will only appear from a point where there is, or has already been, a leaf.

As a final word, I would like to say that the purpose of this book is to supply you with the technical details which you may then use to create whatever designs you have in mind.

The technique itself has been re-formed, and is based on rules which have been used in the last thirty years as applied to botany. Thus, for the first time, the door is wide open for everyone to create miniature trees of their own of any species.

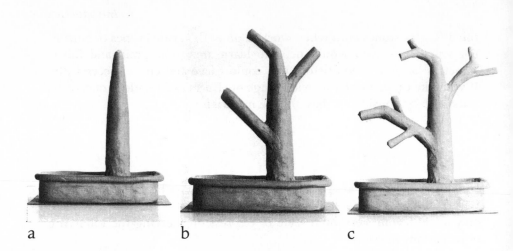

a

b

c

d

e

f

Fig. 2   Modelling (formation of the tree by addition)
(a) the trunk   (b) addition of the main branches   (c) addition of the laterals   (d) addition of the branchlets   (e) addition of the twigs   (f) addition of the leaves, and roots round the trunk

1 · The traditional and the new technique

HINTS ON CULTIVATION IN GENERAL

Before you start, you should realise that a tree, although kept in a container, is not precisely an indoor plant. Most plants can, however, be kept indoors, that is to say in greenhouses (as they often are), where the temperature can be manipulated as required. The important point is that any plant, including our small trees, should be given all it needs.

For the potted tree it is necessary to give it plenty of light; even plenty of sunlight is beneficial as long as we can manage to keep the compost moist. This may mean that you will have to water twice a day if the container is very small or shallow, and stands in full sun during a hot and cloudless summer day. *Remember:* never let the compost become bone-dry.

The tree needs fresh air, but will suffer if exposed to draught. We also have to make sure that the compost contains all the nourishment necessary for healthy growth. Frost can be fatal even to such species which are known to be frost-resistant, because the roots of potted trees are not deep down in frost-free ground, but rather at ground-frost-level. Finally, we have to keep the plant free from pests and diseases.

How do we manage all this with the minimum of effort? The solution for people living in flats is to have two places for the tree. One is a permanent place outside, on the balcony or window-sill, and the other a temporary place indoors, for display. The trees are thus kept most of the time outdoors, and only taken inside for occasional display.

All plants need a rest period or dormant season of some kind—for instance succulent plants will need a spell of complete dryness at some time, deciduous trees should have a rest of two months at least, but coniferous plants can be kept under growing conditions almost all the year round. They will, however, slow down the growing process during the days when there are only a few hours of sunlight.

During the dormant season all species should be kept in a protective shelter, where there is still plenty of light, and no danger of damage from frost. The temperature should be cool, and the drying out of the compost must still be prevented. A temperature around 4°C (38°F) will do very well, and as an approximate average you will be able to manage with one weekly watering. Do not keep the plants in a heated room during winter, or during what is their natural dormant or rest period.

The most common pests and diseases are mildew and aphids (greenfly). Every year new remedies become available and, to avoid confusion, it is best to take a sample of the infected part, or whole tree, to your nursery-man or garden shop, and ask for advice. Always follow the instructions given on the label, and never use a stronger solution than the one recommended. Generally, plants which find all they need in the compost are healthy and more resistant to pests and diseases.

THE TRADITIONAL TECHNIQUE

The Japanese technique makes limited use of the 'dwarfing effect through growing'. As a rule, the growth is only encouraged once in a growing cycle, by stopping the new shoots in the last third of the summer period. The sole purpose of this step is to produce a slightly smaller leaf by the end of summer.

The accent on shaping in the traditional technique lies in wiring. Copper wire is used, over a protective layer of raffia, running in coils around the branch. Another method, that used by professional growers in Japan to gain time, is the art of grafting. A branch with laterals in the first degree (that is, the first sideshoots produced from a main branch) is grafted on to the trunk of a well established root-stock.

This explains the great difference in thickness between branch formation and trunk, which is still noticeable on most of the younger Bonsai in Japan (trees of around an age of 50 years). Flowering trees such as cherries, peaches and plums are started off from cuttings in Japanese nurseries.

When starting to grow a Bonsai from seed, the traditional technique recommends one to begin the actual training of the tree in the second or third year after germination. It is recommended that a healthy plant with a strong stem is established first, after which the specific training for Bonsai can begin.

In the traditional technique one can still see the very strong link with the early beginnings of Bonsai, when plants from the open ground, stunted by nature, were used. However, the tremendous disadvantages here are that the roots have thickened in the same ratio as the trunk, and the capillary roots are too far away from the trunk. Consequently a two-year-old plant has to be pruned back to a point where one is left with the thick parts of the roots close around the trunk. The grower is then faced with the problem of stimulating new growth on old wood, because the roots immediately surrounding the trunk have hardened to the same degree as the trunk. Obviously, this is a very tedious process, and the results are generally poor in comparison to the training of roots on very young seedlings.

The theory of achieving thickness first and then eliminating unwanted material is applied to branch formation as well. A shoot is allowed to grow freely until the finish of the growing season, and then cut back to the desired length. On older, established trees, stopping during the latter part of the growing season is done to encourage smaller secondary growth although, at this late stage, the plant can only produce the first new leaves of the new shoots before growth comes to a seasonal standstill. Hence nothing further is gained than smaller leaves by the time of leaf fall or the rest period.

The traditional technique relies solely on the restriction of root formation as the dwarfing factor. Therefore, the plants are kept in small containers from the very beginning, the reason for this being to re-create the same conditions under which nature produces retarded growth, although the restriction of roots results simultaneously in uneven as well as small growth. The dwarfing effect thus achieved is negligible, and applies to a minority of species only, where the degree of success is only such that a leaf $\frac{1}{10}$th of the original size is obtained.

A further disadvantage of the traditional technique is the uneven growth, as mentioned before, whereby the grower has no positive influence on the growth pattern, and has to be content with what the plant is capable of producing under these stunting conditions. The only two departures from using a small container are when the plant is looking weak and unhealthy, or when a thick trunk is required quickly. When either of these conditions arises, the tree is transplanted to a larger container or the open ground, until the result required has been achieved.

For the type of so-called 'instant Bonsai', use is made of older plants either from the wilds or from the old nursery stocks. Here the procedure can be likened to changing an old-fashioned dress into one of the latest style. The grower must make use of the existing pattern of growth by selective and severe pruning. If there is sufficient material to cut away, the result may prove satisfactory, but if insufficient, additional material has to be produced. Here again, one must remember that old wood does not readily produce new shoots, and so one can therefore appreciate the necessity of relying extensively on grafting, when using the traditional technique. A great quantity of the commercial Bonsai in Japan are established by grafting young material on to a strong trunk with a well-established rootstock.

THE TECHNIQUE OF KAMUTI

Kamuti means 'small tree', in *Shona*, the language of Mashonaland, in Zimbabwe. The Kamuti technique is the system of growing miniature trees in a natural way. The trees are grown under perfect and naturally healthy conditions, and are built up from bottom to top, step by step, adjusted to their natural habit of growth.

The result is not only the rapid production of a miniature tree, but also the production of a shape exactly in accordance with the aims of the grower. The degree of dwarfing of the leaves can be more than $\frac{1}{100}$th of the original size in the case of the large-leaved varieties, whereas $\frac{1}{10}$th is considered the ultimate amount of reduction for the Japanese system.

When raising miniature trees by the Kamuti technique, we are not working against nature to achieve dwarf characteristics; on the contrary, we are working with the help of nature.

Other advantages of the Kamuti technique are:

1. All training is done while the plant is young, hence all pruning will be done on green shoots, which in turn leaves a tree without scars.
2. The tree will be established before reaching maturity, and this is the ideal method of obtaining dwarfed characteristics.

3. The dwarfing process does not rely on root-pruning. A Kamuti only needs root-pruning because we are going to plant the tree in a small container.

4. Trunk, main branches, branchlets and twigs will thicken in relation to each other harmoniously, in the same way as they do in their big brethren.

2 · Miniature trees, their size and shape

HOW TO COPY A TREE IN MINIATURE

If we try to copy in miniature a natural tree with its hundreds of branches and twigs, we shall arrive at a plant looking very much like a shrub (see plate 1). Instead, we have to create the image with less material. Therefore, to avoid density, we shall have only three to five main branches coming from the trunk, and lateral shoots in the first and further degrees should increase only gradually in number. As a hard and fast rule: never let three lateral shoots start from one point; the fork is the better alternative.

Care must be taken to avoid crossing lines, they irritate and distract from the overall flow; the eye registers crossed lines like a net, which in turn reduces the impression of depth. The space between branches is important, too. Try to prevent any symmetry and parallel lines in these spaces (see plates 2–4).

THE SIZE

As with all other features, the size is entirely the choice of the grower. You can have a tree 2 feet or 2 inches high—it is as you wish. All you need is a mental image, a target, according to which you have to adjust all your calculations (see fig. 3).

For example, if you want to build up a tree of about 2 feet tall, you will need the lowest main branch at 7–11 inches from the soil level. If your tree is meant to be only 4 inches high, then the lowest main branch should be at about 2 inches above the soil.

This may sound very difficult, but in fact it is very easy, for the plant is going to help you. All that is needed from you is the guiding hand.

The trees which make the most impact are around 2 feet tall, although

24

Plate 1 *Ficus religiosa,* Peepul tree; a too dense trunk and branch formation cannot be copied in miniature as it would result in the plant looking like a shrub

Plate 2 *Schizolobium excelsum*; here five main branches radiate from one point

Plate 3 *Cupressus torulosa,* Bhutan cypress; a formal tree, where only the outlines speak

Plate 4 *Jacaranda mimosaefolia*; the lines of this tree wind gracefully upwards, gradually merging softly into a widely spreading canopy

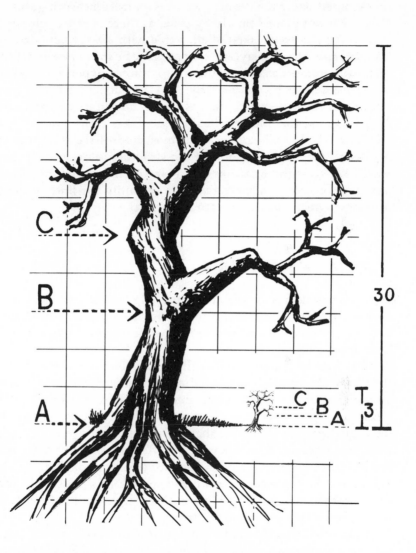

Fig. 3 When sculpturing small trees, all we have to do is to decrease the dimensions of the single elements. If a tree is to be only 1/10th of the size of a normal one, the lines between A and B, and B and C must be 1/10th of the normal length

the favoured size in the Western world is for trees measuring about 1 foot. This size is not guided purely by taste, as there are three circumstances stimulating this trend. First of all, a tree with a height of 2 feet needs a fairly big space for display, and cannot easily be shifted around. Secondly, a Bonsai container matching this size is rather expensive, and in most Western countries hard to come by. And last but not least, a tall tree needs strong and thick elements, such as trunks and branches, and achieving this, if you use the traditional technique, takes many years.

In a nutshell, a miniature tree is most impressive when the eye can register all the single elements of the structure at once. Well calculated spaces between the branches will give the impression of observing a normal sized tree from close range. It is mainly the lines of the branch formation which make a tree attractive to the eye.

WHAT MAKES A TREE

Since our problem is an optical one, we only have to consider the appearance of the tree. All we want is to reconstruct a tree of small dimensions. Basically a trunk and a crown are the two features that set a tree visually apart from other plants.

When you look down from a hill into a valley you may notice that all trees look almost alike. Masses of green, rounded in various shapes, is all one can see—from this angle, even trees look like shrubs. It is only when you see a single tree from ground level at close range, that the individual one shows its real shape, character and age.

No two trees are alike. They are as different as human faces, and each one has its own personality. To give our trees individuality, we have to make use of the features we noticed when taking a close look. These are the main branches, twigs and leaves. Older trees have part of their thick root system exposed around the trunk.

So, we now know that a tree is not just a trunk and a crown. The whole pattern is a structure of various single elements, each one in its proper place.

1. The trunk = the centrepiece of our structure
2. The main branches = added character

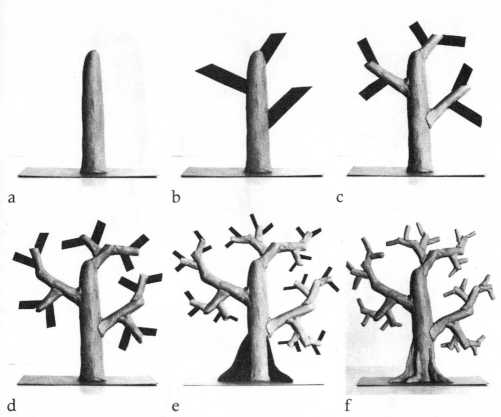

a   b   c

d   e   f

Fig. 4   What makes a tree   (a) the trunk   (b) the main branches   (c) laterals (sideshoots) of the first degree   (d) laterals of the second degree   (e) laterals of the third degree, and so on   (f) roots

3. The laterals in the first, second and third degrees, etc., are elements to express grace and beauty
7. The foliage = a gentle frame
5. The roots = an indication of age (see figs. 4a–f)

Although the main branches are actually the lateral shoots in the first degree, counting from the trunk, I prefer to classify them as main branches, because they are the most powerful medium for expressing character, age and personality.

We have to bear in mind when sculpturing our little trees that the foliage must be used sparsely, in order to give us a good view of the

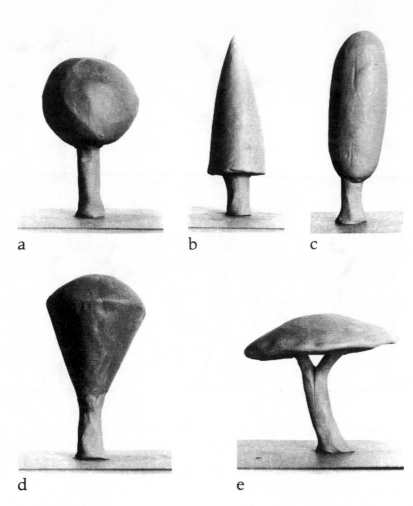

Fig. 5   Primary shapes   (a) the ball   (b) the pyramid   (c) the column   (d) the broom   (e) the umbrella

branch formation. Think of human hair, and how much it can alter the personal appearance according to how it is arranged. Often we go as far as judging a person simply by the way in which the hair is done.

SHAPES, BASIC

There are only five basic shapes (see figs. 5a–e) and, because of their simple, rather monotonous outline, they are very seldom reproduced in miniature.

The ball. Many trees belong to this class and develop such a form when they are standing free in the open.

The pyramid. The Christmas tree has this distinct shape. Cypresses of various species show the same pattern, sometimes with a rather elongated tip.

The column. Here the Lombardy poplar is a clear example.

The broom. Many of the smaller growing trees spread their branches in this way.

The umbrella. A shape that is most clearly found among the acacias of South Africa.

The simplicity of line of these five basic shapes, which are mere outlines, is very easy to achieve and as an experiment, it might be worth a try. After all, these are nature's true shapes.

SHAPES, VARIED

The possibilities in variation are almost endless (see figs. 6a–e). The rounded shape can only be indicated by some foliage; the skeleton of trunk and branches is the main attraction. The generally-avoided broom shape can be interesting, when the whole formation is split up on various levels.

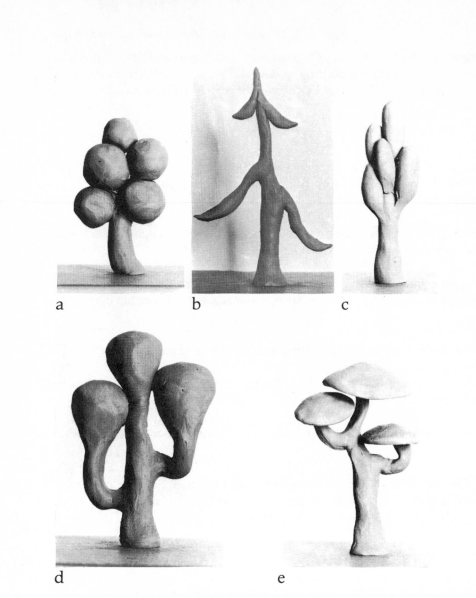

a   b   c

d   e

Fig. 6 Variation of primary shapes (a) the ball (b) the pyramid (c) the column (d) the broom (e) the umbrella

Even the history of the tree can be determined. For instance, a tree which has grown in the depths of the forest will not have developed any laterals (side branches) on the lower part of the trunk, because of the lack of light and space.

Next time you drive into the country, keep your eyes open, and you will get many ideas for new shapes of miniature trees.

SHAPES, EXTREME

Certain styles of potted trees can only be grouped here, because their structure is purely artistic, and bears little relation to naturally growing shapes. There are the kinds where very few branches have been used, and the trunk is mostly the one and only focal point. Some cascade over the rim of the container far below soil level. Others look like skilfully-made ornaments, with their branches perfectly placed.

I think you will now realise how wide is the range of design for potted trees, and how many possibilities are open to you. From the broom shape to the abstract sculpture in living wood, the field is yours to experiment with (see fig. 27i).

3 · Growth characteristics of trees and shrubs

Trees multiply by means of seed produced after flowering. When ripe the seed is shed on to the ground, where moisture and warmth together stimulate the germination and birth of a new tree. The viability of seed is limited and varies with each species from a few days to two or more years.

Right from the beginning a young plant, a seedling, shows three features which are important when talking in terms of potted trees:

1. The roots—the support or anchor
2. The trunk—the centrepiece
3. The foliage—the ornamentation

LEAVES

Let us consider the leaves first. There are three different ways in which leaves are produced on the stem:

(a) Alternate; single
(b) Opposite; in pairs
(c) Circular; three or more at one level (see fig. 7)

In the axil of any leaf there is at least one dormant bud which can produce a new shoot. Therefore the rule we have to remember is that:

We can expect a new shoot at such a position where there is a leaf, or where there has been a leaf.

Some trees and shrubs produce new shoots at these points year after year. These are the ones we use for hedges. Many other trees are reluctant to produce sideshoots on old wood, mainly those whose top has already reached a certain strength. This can be a great handicap when working on stunted plants, collected from open ground, or from old nursery stock.

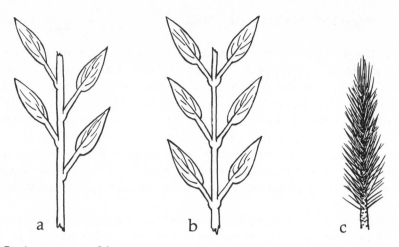

Fig. 7   Arrangement of leaves on stem   (a) alternate   (b) in pairs   (c) circular

On hedges we can clearly see the reaction of plants to the routine clipping or trimming (also called pruning or stopping). When the growing ends of the shoots are cut off, dormant buds in the leaf axils become active and burst out into new shoots.

This is another rule we shall make use of when shaping our trees.

THE ROOTS

The root system is slightly different. Roots have cells which can produce laterals all over the surface, but the readiness to send out laterals varies with the species. However, at the very early stage of the seedling, the majority of plants will produce new roots fairly rapidly when there is a need for it.

Here again, we can stimulate new growth by pruning. When we cut off the growing tip of a single root, the cut end cannot continue to grow and lengthen. The alternative is for the plant to send out secondary roots or laterals from the sides.

By using this technique we can build up a dense root system close around the trunk, instead of having a long and stringy root formation, gradually getting further and further away from the trunk, and becoming more and more difficult to deal with.

GROWING HABITS OF TREES

From the moment a seed germinates, a tree starts to grow, and goes on growing until it dies. In other words, the size of a tree is greater every year, although the ratio of size to age lessens as the tree becomes older. Even the oldest tree not only produces new leaves, but extends the branch formation as well, as long as it lives. A tree never reaches a point where it stands absolutely still in its growing process. For this reason, even the oldest Bonsai must be periodically pruned to retain their appearance. Furthermore, a grower can improve on an old tree, as is still done on even the oldest and most famous examples of Bonsai in Japan.

The juvenile stage. From the seed, the first root emerges and finds its way down into the soil, while at the same time the cotyledons (seed leaves), imbedded in the seed, swell up to such a point that they split open the protective skin of the seed. They are then raised into the light on the extending stem and start right away to act as digestive tools. With the help of light absorbed by the leaves minerals are turned into plant nourishment. You will notice that the leaves are always turned towards the source of light (see fig. 8).

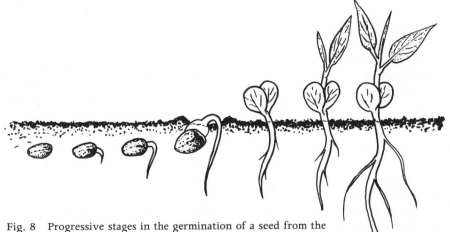

Fig. 8 Progressive stages in the germination of a seed from the production of the first root, to the emergence of the true leaves

The single root produced at the beginning is not enough to maintain the plant's development, and the seedling therefore grows laterals, or capillary roots. These are always thinner than the first one, and act mainly as feeder roots. Their ability to stabilise the plant in the soil is negligible in comparison to the main roots.

All this activity takes place in a layer of soil not deeper than 2–3 inches.

At a later stage, when the centre or tap root has reached deeper soil, these first capillary roots will die off. Yet, tiny as they are, they have the capacity to grow, thicken and produce lateral roots like any other root. Let us therefore have a look at the structure of a root and its capabilities.

The characteristics which are important to us when sculpturing little trees, are easy to remember.

1. The root which is still light in colour and has not yet acquired a woody protective layer on the outside, is young and easily broken; it takes in plant food through the walls of certain cells on the outside layer. A plant should always be left with a quantity of such young capillary roots, to make sure that it can survive and continue to grow after root-pruning and repotting.

2. The root also has cells with the ability to divide. These cells are all over all roots, but with slight variations in arrangement, for example in lines (as on some plants with tuberous roots), and not indiscriminately. In all plants, the ability to stimulate the growth of new cells is always strongest at the tip of the root, the most forward end. By means of such continuous cell-production at the tip, the root grows longer and longer. At the same time, the plant can activate new cells along the line to bring out laterals which proceed in exactly the same way as the leading tip. And these laterals, in turn, can do the same, because they all carry cells having the necessary faculty.

For different reasons, the plant can stimulate cells to grow into laterals, all with the one aim of absorbing the most from the soil. The adherence to the soil, or the grip, is a fringe benefit, so to speak. A plant never puts out roots for this purpose alone, the reason being that the leader passes through a layer of soil which is moister than the rest, or a layer which is richer in nutrient minerals.

The most important point for us to remember, however, is that: when

39

we take off the growing tip of a root, it cannot continue to grow in the same direction and will instead stimulate some cells along the line towards the trunk to erupt into laterals. Now, because of this, we have a chance to establish a root system exactly as we would wish for a Bonsai. It will show the divided and split-up network of roots that an old tree produces, but in a much smaller area; or better still, in perfect relation to our little tree.

A more than usually split-up root-formation is stimulated by using a high percentage of coarse sandy substance in the growing medium. In such a mixture, the roots have difficulty in attaching themselves to the soil particles, and subsequently will produce more laterals than they would do in a soil with a high content of fine clay particles. We shall make use of this point also, in the composition of our potting mixture.

The mature stage below ground. The roots closest to the trunk and leading away from it, are the first to harden. Such roots still have cells which can divide to produce laterals, although the plant uses these only in a state of emergency. In general, one can put it like this: old wood is reluctant to produce new shoots and when it does, it is never done as spontaneously as on fresh green shoots, and it never happens in quantity—it is the exception on which we cannot rely.

The mature stage above ground. The first parts of the seedling to break through the soil are the cotyledons. They never look like the true leaf of the species and are in many cases shaped rather like discs. All growth thereafter starts at the point where the cotyledons join the little stem.

From there a shoot evolves which will bring out the first leaves. We are speaking now of the first true leaves—the cotyledons are not, they are the seed leaves. The leaves will appear, either alternately, one after the other, or in pairs, two at the same level on opposite sides of the stem, or they may be produced in a ring, that is, so that there are more than two leaves at the same level.

Some trees need to grow to a certain height before they will put out laterals. As a general rule, it is worthwhile remembering that a tree will put out new shoots, laterals, one degree further every year. It may, however, happen that a warm and sunny autumn encourages a plant to produce a second batch of new shoots and leaves, and even flowers,

Plate 5   *Celtis africana* ($8\frac{1}{2}''$, 3 years)

Plate 6 *Pinus patula* (24″, 5½ years)

which you may have seen. This usually occurs when there has been a colder spell in late summer.

The normal behaviour of trees is that, in spring, a new shoot with new leaves is produced, and in the following spring a year later, new shoots come out from the points where the new leaves grew. In the years thereafter, new shoots will again come out of the leaf axils of the previous year's shoots. From this behaviour, we learn that every new shoot has:

(a) cells to perpetuate growth
(b) cells to produce leaves
(c) cells for growing flowers and seed

We have to remember that cells with the ability to form new shoots are only at positions where there is, or there has been, a leaf. If the growing tips of young new shoots are removed by browsing animals or destroyed by pests or diseases, the plant still has the ability to activate dormant cells on the old wood, at any position where there was once a leaf.

The same principle applies here as with the roots: old wood is normally reluctant to stimulate new growth. New green shoots quite readily push out new laterals when the growing tip has been removed and the plant is healthy and not undergoing dormancy. This again is a characteristic which will help us when shaping a tree.

All trees need water, light and nourishment, the last-named being mainly in the soil. The basic foods a plant needs are: nitrogen, phosphorus and potassium, together with the trace elements, so called because minute quantities only are needed by the plant. Water is necessary as a carrier of food within the plant. Light is needed for the process of digestion, for in the leaves the minerals and elements are converted into plant food, with the help of light (photosynthesis).

Lack of light during the growing season will result in weak and pale growth, which if normal water is supplied, will also be leggy. Since we are trying to obtain the exact opposite, it follows that we must give our trees as much sunlight as possible during the active time of the year, when we will be rewarded with sturdy growth.

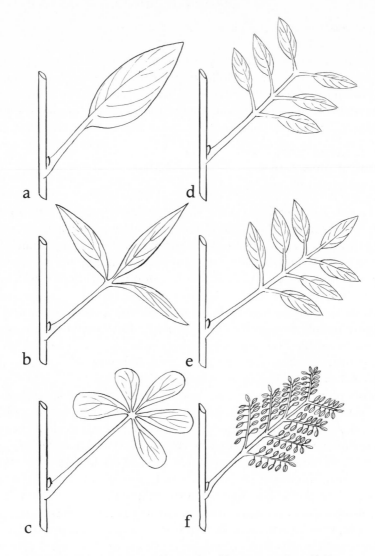

Fig. 9 Leaf structures (a) single (b) compound, trifoliate (threefold) (c) compound, digitate or palmate (finger-like) (d) compound, paripinnate (with an equal number of leaflets, no terminal one) (e) compound, imparipinnate (feather-like with an odd terminal leaflet) (f) compound, bipinnate (feather-like to two degrees)

TYPES OF LEAF

Basically, there are two groups of leaves: the single leaf, and the compound leaf. The single leaf is the less confusing, although there are many variations on this type. If one has no experience of leaf structures, it is advisable to investigate and understand the complexities of the compound leaf (see fig. 9).

The trifoliate leaf is composed of three leaflets; the digitate or palmate leaf has more than three leaflets radiating from one point. Examining pinnate and bipinnate leaves, at first glance one would think each consisted of a collection of shoots with opposite leaves attached. Yet the single units are in fact leaflets attached to the leaf stalk (the petiole), and there are no reproducing buds in the axil of a leaflet. Only at the point where the whole leaf is attached to the stem are one or more buds present, which in time can produce new lateral shoots.

Before working with a new species, it is necessary to familiarise oneself with the characteristics of its leaves, so as to know exactly where to find the axillary bud that will produce the shoot for the next step (see fig. 9, for different leaf types).

Position of leaves. All single and compound leaves appear in one of three different positions. In group 1 the leaves are alternate, not opposite. For us, it means we can expect a new shoot only at alternate points (see fig. 7a). In the second group the leaves are opposite, in a pair at the same level. Here we can make use of two shoots or branches at the same height, lying opposite each other (see fig. 7b). In group 3 the leaves are arranged in a circular manner. More than two leaves will be on the same level, and consequently we may have more than two shoots at the same height. This, indeed, is never wanted, but it does give us more choice of the direction in which to grow a shoot (see fig. 7c).

The kind of design that can be constructed according to the growing habits of the species, alternate, opposite, or circular leaf arrangement, can be seen in fig. 10.

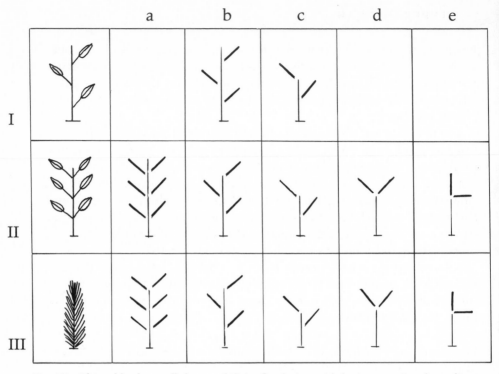

Fig. 10 This table shows all the possibilities for design with various species, depending on their leaf positions, whether they are alternate (I), opposite (II) or circular (III).   (a) more than one fork on one line   (b) more than one alternate shoot from one line   (c) two alternate shoots from one line   (d) the simple fork   (e) a fork used as one shoot and one leader   For species with their leaves in alternate positions, the variations in structure are limited, nevertheless the growing characteristics of these species, the continuous change in the direction of the lines, is exactly what we are aiming at.

4 · The Kamuti technique

GERMINATION

Do not be afraid of raising plants from seeds. They generally germinate quite easily; nature makes most of them this way to ensure survival of the species (see fig. 8). Most failures arise from being over careful. For the first trials, get your seed from a reputable dealer. Later, when you know more about the germination behaviour of different species, you may collect your own seed.

In the framework of this book it would be an impossible task to list the germination details of the individual species. Some are best sown immediately after ripening, some need a dormant period, while others have a double dormancy and need a cold spell before they will germinate. Reputable seedsmen will always supply seed which is suited to the coming season.

Sow the seeds at the right time, that is, in the spring, and never place them too close together. Leave enough space for the first leaves to spread without coming into contact with each other.

Use a soil mixture which is rather on the sandy side, never consisting mainly of clay; this will ensure that the drainage is good. The John Innes seed compost is also very suitable. Cover the seed with a layer of the compost, only as thick as the seed is in diameter, put through a fine sieve. Try to keep the moisture of the compost as constant as possible, never too wet and never too dry. The same applies to the temperature—keep it as constant as you can manage, not hot during the day and cool at night.

This might sound a little bit difficult to achieve, but it really is not. For germination, all seeds do best with the temperature a little on the warm side, about 24–27°C (75–80°F). The actual process of germination needs no light whatsoever. Because of this, we may cover the seed box, so as to retain moisture, with a piece of cardboard or black plastic sheeting. However, as soon as the seedling breaks through the soil, the protective cover must be removed, because the tender plants will want light or, better still, sunshine. Gradually, over a week or so, we expose the seed box more and more to the sunlight.

THE GROWING CONTAINER

The growing container is the receptacle for your plant while it is being trained in the initial stages. It is used only to establish the miniature tree. We can use almost anything for this, boxes, tins, plastic containers or beds in the open lined with plastic sheets. When using a tin, remove the rim before planting. When using plastic bags or pockets, use the black ones only, to protect the soil from light.

All containers must have ample drainage. It is better to have a few big holes than many small ones. If the diameter of the drainage holes is more than $\frac{1}{2}$ inch (13 mm), we place a piece of acrylic fibre gauze over it, to prevent the soil from being washed out.

Make sure your container has its greatest width at the top. Pots which are wider at the base than on top, or which become wider in the middle, will present you with a problem when repotting.

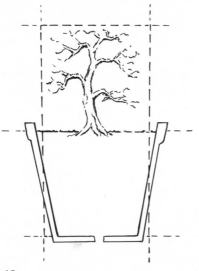

Fig. 11   The growing container should hold at least as much soil as the total volume of the final tree will amount to. It would be even better if the roots can be given double the room

The size of the growing container, or rather the volume of soil, should be at least in direct relation to the final volume of the tree you want to grow, for instance, 1:1. If you aim for a tree of about one square foot in area, the soil should be at least one square foot as well (see fig. 11). More soil still will result not only in faster growth, but better and more even growth also. We only limit the root system to make a later transfer into a shallow container possible.

HOW TO START A MINIATURE TREE

The ideal age to start a plant for a potted tree is as a seedling that has just developed the first true leaves after the cotyledons. For species with alternate or paired leaves, the plant should not be taller than 1–2 inches. At this stage the majority of seedlings show the same root formation, regardless of species. Even the plants which later show an extended tap root are, at the early stage, supported by a few capillary roots.

Here we start our first training. We take the seedling out of the pot, and carefully shake the soil off the roots. From now until re-planting, we must be careful not to let the roots become dry at all in, for instance, sun or wind. As all roots of the tender seedling have to be stopped, we then take away the growing tip of every single root. As a reaction to our pruning, the plant will then send out laterals. What we gain is a denser root system close around the trunk (see figs. 12a–c, 13a, 14a, 15a).

Now we plant the seedling in the growing container, and keep it in the shade until we see new leaves developing. Gradually, over two or three days, we then bring it into full sunshine.

BUILDING UP THE TOP GROWTH

Having done all this to the seedling, and planted it in the growing container, we can expect fairly rapid growth. Now comes the time for sculpturing, and we must bear in mind our aims as far as height and shape of the future tree are concerned. The following notes are illustrated in figs. 12d–p and 13b–i, and it will be helpful to refer to these as the text is read.

a

b

c

d

e

f

g

h

i

j

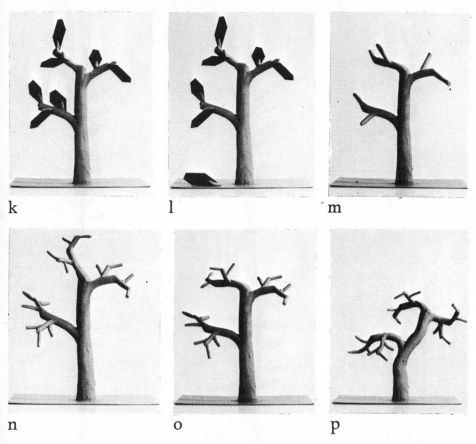

k   l   m

n   o   p

Fig. 12   Step by step build-up of a tree with leaves produced alternately   (a) young seedling with the first true leaves completely developed   (b) all the roots are pruned (stopped) at the points indicated; the tap-root (centre) is stopped just under the lowest capillary root   (c) reaction to root-pruning: a much denser root system after some weeks in the growing container   (d) the seedling some weeks later; note the alternate arrangement of the leaves   (e) the position of three main branches has been chosen, and the seedling is now stopped immediately above the point where the highest main branch is required   (f) reaction to stopping: the buds in the leaf axils are induced to shoot   (g) all unwanted buds are now removed, together with the leaves at these points   (h) the three buds have now grown into shoots bearing leaves (these shoots will form the main branches)   (i) choose the number of laterals required on the main branches and also their positions; then stop each shoot above the lateral required to be nearest to the end   (j) appearance after the stopping done at (i)   (k) reaction to stopping: leaf axil buds begin to grow (as in f)   (l) again remove the unwanted buds together with the leaves (as in g); here only one is removed   (m) the first degree laterals on the main branches, grown and then stopped, here shown without the leaves for clarity   (n) after stopping the laterals of the first degree, the second degree laterals form   (o) the beginning of shaping the tree   (p) stiffness in appearance is further eliminated by shaping to the third dimension

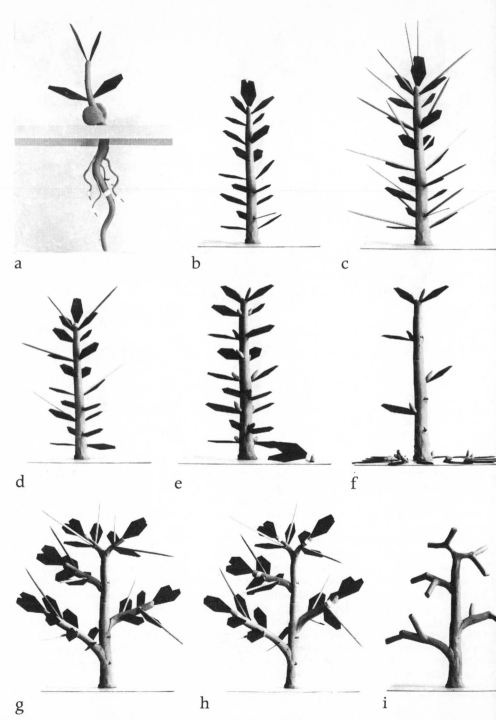

a

b

c

d

e

f

g

h

i

First, we let the seedling grow to the height at which it has the number of leaves we need for our main branches. If it is a species in which the space between the leaves is such that the branches will be produced closer together than you require, you can let the seedling grow to the height at which it has not only the requisite number of leaves, but leaves at the right points as well. The latter will mainly apply for a tree with the lowest branch starting higher than 5 inches above soil-level.

At this stage we take off the growing tip, that is, we stop the seedling just above the highest leaf; this will give us the position of the highest main branch in due course.

Whenever we remove a growing-tip from a shoot, the plant cannot continue to grow in its original direction (usually vertical). Consequently the dormant buds in the leaf-axils are activated, that is, the ones which can produce new shoots. The final results of our stopping will be a seedling with a vertical stem and laterals coming out from the sides at all points where there was a leaf.

If you were aiming at a taller tree, and you had to retain more leaves than the number of main branches needed, you can now remove all unwanted shoots. The same applies for species with leaves in pairs. Remember: three lines coming from the same point are considered un-

---

Fig. 13 (opposite) Step by step build-up of a tree with leaves produced in pairs (a) seedling with the first true leaves. The growing tips are removed from all the root ends, and the seedling planted in a growing container (b) the seedling after some weeks in the growing container. Note: all the leaves are opposite, in pairs (c) at all the points indicated we can expect a lateral shoot to be produced. The choice for positioning the main branches is up to the grower (d) five positions have been selected for the main branches, three at different levels, and two to produce a simple fork at the top. Stop the plant immediately above the point where the highest main branch is required (e) reaction to stopping: the buds in the leaf axils begin to grow (f) unwanted buds are rubbed off, together with the leaves at these points (g) the main branches have grown and produced leaves, and on these we choose the number and the position of the laterals of the first degree. On the three lower branches we have chosen an alternate position for the laterals, and on the top two branches forming a fork, we choose two laterals at the same level to form another fork (h) stop each main branch just above the lateral required, without damaging the buds in the leaf axils (i) laterals of the first degree have now formed, shown here without the leaves for clarity. Laterals of the second and further degrees are built up as in the previous stages

sightly. The unwanted shoots are best removed at the earliest oppor-
tunity, as soon as you can see the new shoot developing in the leaf-axil.

When the new shoots have produced their first leaves, it is time to
remove the old leaves of the first stage.

After this we are presented with the basic constituents of our future
tree, the trunk and the main branches. From now on the technique is
repeated on every new shoot. We let the new lateral grow until it has
the number of leaves we want for laterals, or until we have leaves at
the positions where we want laterals in the next stage. The shoot is
stopped then, like the previous one, above the last leaf. The reaction will
be the same as before.

New shoots will appear at all the leaf-axils and we are presented with a
structure which is already much more like a tree. When the first leaves
on these latest new shoots are there, we can remove the older leaves of
the previous stage.

Our tree has now reached the third stage, showing the trunk, the main
branches and the laterals in the first degree. To bring out the laterals in
the second and any further degree, you proceed exactly as in the last
two stages. It is entirely up to you where you densify the structure with
more branch-formation, or where you gain height or drop the lines. If
you want to come down, you simply remove shoots which are pointing
upwards, and leave only those pointing down to grow.

Remember as a hard and fast rule: never let a shoot grow longer in any
direction than you actually need for appearance. Firstly, long straight
lines are not becoming. Secondly, the diversion from the completely
straight line indicates age to the eyes.

Since the growing seasons (spring and summer) vary considerably in
the different parts of the world and one summer is not like another, the
stage of build-up one can reach during one season will differ from place
to place and year to year. The altitude of your location will have some
effect in extreme positions, for example mountain areas.

The minimum you can achieve as an average in areas up to 300 metres
(approx. 1,000 feet) above sea level is indicated in the Table which follows,
although this can be increased by up to two stages with simple aids, as
you will find in the section headed 'Extended Growing Season', which
follows this Table:

TABLE SHOWING RATE OF BUILD-UP

1. In areas between 55 and 65°Lat. N or S   2 stages
2. In areas between 45 and 55°Lat. N or S   3 stages
3. In areas between 0 and 45°Lat. N or S   4 stages

EXTENDED GROWING SEASON

The length of the growing season has an influence on the speed of your sculpturing with living material. This is because it is only during the warm spells that your plant will produce the material needed for shaping. It is therefore advisable to extend the warm period, or rather, make use of all the sunshine there is. There is a very simple way of retaining the warmth of sunshine in early spring and keeping away the cool air, and that is by using an ordinary plastic bag fixed over a structure of wire; alternatively polythene sheeting can be used to provide a tent with the dimensions of a small hothouse. However, whether small or large, you must make provision for aeration holes, so that air may gently circulate. The inside of the plastic should not be covered permanently with condensation, which is a symptom of insufficient ventilation within the shelter.

Another way of getting more out of one season is by starting germination in very early spring in a warm place indoors, and then putting the young seedlings, well protected from the cold air, in the early spring sun. You should make sure that your miniature hothouse retains some of the warmth of the day during the night. This will not be the case if it has a small internal volume, and the alternative will be to take the whole growing unit indoors while the nights are still cold. The same applies for the late season. Autumn can be made use of for encouraging new growth, when a fairly constant warmth, together with sunlight, is present.

RAPID DWARFING

Cypress and juniper are very suitable for this technique. The procedure is very much like cutting a hedge. The training starts when the seedling has reached about half the final height envisaged. At this stage, begin to

Plate 7   *Cupressus macrocarpa*, Monterey cypress (24″, 7 years)

Plate 8   *Acer buergeranum*, Tridend maple (21″, 7 years)

trim back all the shoots to the shape of a small pyramid (see fig. 33, page 98). Then increase the size of the pyramid gradually by adding layer after layer. The shoots will double and treble as you continue, and the plant will become denser with every stage. For the root pruning, the time to do it and the amount to prune are as for all other trees.

The tree is planted into the final display container when the complete density required has been obtained.

TREES WITH MORE THAN TWO LEAVES AT THE SAME LEVEL (circular, ring-leaved)

These are evergreen trees with leaves shaped mostly like needles, pine, spruce (*Picea*), cedar and fir (*Abies*). As a rule, these plants will produce new shoots only close to the cut which has stopped a shoot. We will never get new shoots from all the remaining leaf axils, as we do on vigorous deciduous plants, so we have to apply a different method of build-up for all such species.

It is necessary to think in terms of forking. We do not have to count the number of leaves or, rather, needles. The seedling is stopped when it has reached the height where we want the first and lowest branch to be (see figs. 14c and d). If you want a trunk with a length of 5 inches to the lowest main branch, you stop the seedling just above this point.

As a reaction to your stopping, the dormant buds in the leaf axils closest to the cut will be activated into growth, and new shoots will appear (fig. 14e). The number will vary with the species; it can be up to five as happens with the five-needled pine species (*Pinus montezumae, P. monticola*). Every seedling in a normal healthy condition will produce two to three new shoots, and in exceptional cases even one or two from the lower parts of the stem (figs. 14f and g).

If you find more than two new shoots at the top, remove the excess as soon as you can recognize them. Of the two remaining shoots, one is meant to be the lowest main branch while the other is still to be the leader, the trunk.

For the next stopping, the desired point for branching is the decisive factor for stopping, not the number of leaves. Since one line is still meant to be the trunk you will probably let it grow a little longer than the other one, which is supposed to be the lowest main branch (figs. 14h and i). After stopping at the right height, you allow only two shoots to develop further, so forming a fork (fig. 14j).

For the stopping of these new shoots, the distance is again the only point affecting your decision, although you have to bear in mind that the lowest part that you are working on is already a branch, and that the other can be shaped as two main branches or as one main branch and the leader or trunk (figs. 14k and l, see also figs. 15b–g).

Whichever choice you decide will give the best results, you should remember when choosing that it is the length of the parts in relation to each other that will give each tree its individuality. In this context, have a look back at 'What makes a tree', on p. 30.

As you will have realised, the range of variations is endless, and really anything you have in mind is possible. All that is needed is to calculate the space up to the next forking required, and then stop a shoot at that place. And do remember to shorten the intervals more and more, the farther you get away from the trunk; again, see 'What makes a tree'.

Since these species are evergreen and tend to carry their leaves for two and three years it is advisable to remove the old needles, the ones from the previous step, as soon as the new shoot has born new needles (see fig. 14g).

When conifers are to be stopped, pruning is never done as a real cut. Instead, on green material (soft), we separate the growing tip from the supporting stem without damaging any of the needles.

SECOND ROOT-PRUNING

The first root-pruning is done on the very young seedling, just when it has reached the stage where it has developed two or three leaves (see p. 49). It is then planted in the growing container, when the plant has ample space to expand the root system.

In the first year, the second root-pruning is done at about the beginning of the last third of the growing season. This would be the end of July and the beginning of August in the Northern Hemisphere, and the end of December and the start of January in the Southern Hemisphere. At this stage, the plants of most cultivated trees will show us a root formation composed of two different-looking structures.

a   b   c

d   e   f

Fig. 14   Step by step build-up of a species with more than two leaves at the same level (circular arrangement)   (a) a young pine seedling. Stop every single root as indicated, to stimulate a dense root system, and plant at once in a growing container   (b) seedling after some time in the growing container   (c) stop the seedling just above the point where the lowest main branches are required. Be careful to cut the stem only, and not the leaves   (d) seedling after stopping   (e) on pines, new shoots generally only grow close to the stopping point. Here two have appeared at about the same level   (f) sometimes the plant may produce new shoots lower down, mainly doing this when the seedling is still less than 6 inches (15 cm) tall. Here, we have gained one lower shoot which we shall be able to use with advantage in the final image   (g) when the leaves on the new shoots have fully

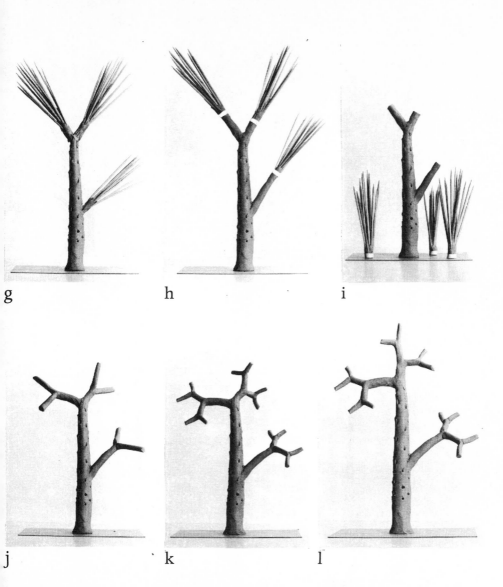

g

h

i

j

k

l

developed, the leaves of the previous stage can always be removed; in this case it is the leaves on the trunk   (h) let the shoot grow up to the point where you would like to see the next forking point. The length of each line is your choice; here three different stages are indicated   (i) the trunk and the main branches after stopping. The leaves have been omitted for clarity   (j) two new shoots at the end of each main branch are used for the laterals of the first degree, each forming a simple fork (k) in the next stage two shoots are added again—these are the laterals of the second degree   (l) here there is a variation: the main branch on the right hand side at the top has been trained vertical to follow the line of the trunk. The same training is applied to one top lateral of the first degree, and repeated with one lateral of the second degree (see also diagrammatic representation, figs. 15 and 31)

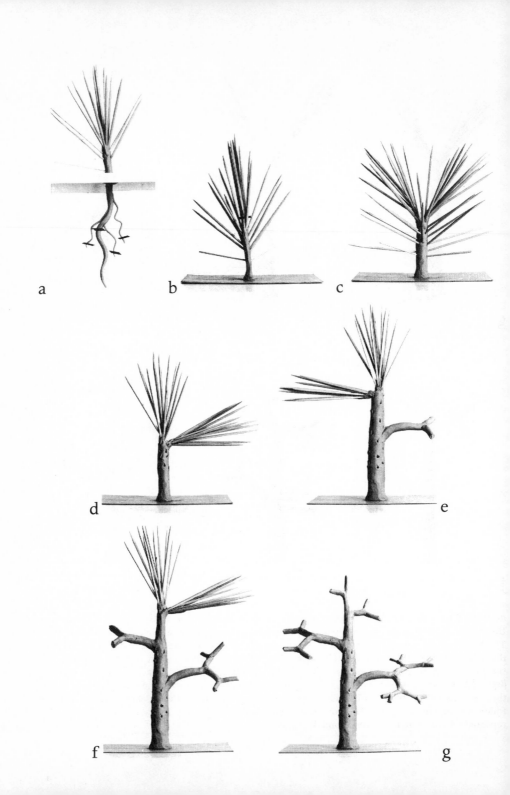

a

b

c

d

e

f

g

On top, around the trunk, we find a dense nest of mainly thin roots with the ability to feed the plant. This cluster has grown as a direct result of our first root-stopping while still a seedling. Secondly, we find five to eight roots, slightly thicker, coming from within the mat of fine roots at the base of the seedling, and growing almost vertically down, towards the base of the container. These roots hardly ever show a split-up formation on their upper parts—only when they reach the bottom of the container do they form laterals. Some vigorous plants can form a lower ball of roots as big as the upper one.

If we have a root formation on top which can hold the soil together, we can cut off all the long, string-like roots. To do this, turn the root-ball upside down in your hand and cut these long roots off as far up as possible, but leave the part from which laterals have appeared. All the other, thinner roots are shortened in length by one-third. If the plant has already produced a dense root-ball on top, you simply shrink the ball by one-third. Just cut away one-third all round and from the under-side.

There are very few species among the cultivated ones which are slow to produce a good ball of fibrous roots, but you may come across them when you start experimenting with indigenous plants which are not normally to be found in your nurseries. In such cases, where your plant shows only a stringy root system, with very few laterals developing in

---

Fig. 15 (*opposite*) Step by step build-up, using one shoot and one leader (a) start with a seedling, prune the roots in the usual way, and plant in a growing container (b) stop just above the point where the lowest main branch is wanted (c) only two new shoots are left to grow (d) one shoot is used as a main branch, the other as the leader, following the line of the trunk (e) of the resultant new shoots, two are used for first degree laterals on the main branch, here forming a simple fork. One of the two shoots at the end of the leader will be the second main branch, while the other is trained vertically to continue as the leader (f) at the next stage, the lowest main branch (right) will produce the laterals of the second degree. The second main branch (left) produces laterals of the first degree. At the top one shoot is again used for a main branch (the third), and the other shoot continues the line as a leader (g) one step further: the lowest main branch with laterals of the third degree, the second main branch (left) with laterals of the second degree, and the third main branch from the bottom has laterals of the first degree. The two new shoots at the top have been handled as before (see also fig. 31)

spite of the early root-pruning it received when it was still a seedling, it is best to shorten each root only by one-third. This applies both to the long ones and remaining laterals. *Remember:* when you replant it, every root should have been stopped, that is, the growing tip should have been removed from every end.

REPLANTING

Before replanting, the container should be filled with fresh compost to about one-third of its capacity. The reduced root-ball is then placed on

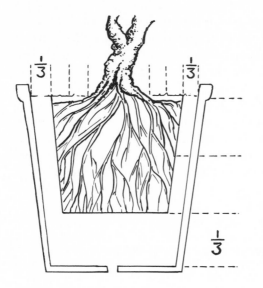

Fig. 16   When root-pruning plants from the growing container, one-third of the volume, roots and soil, is removed. The ball of the remaining two-thirds is replanted, and the missing third is replaced with fresh compost

it in the desired position, and the space round the root-ball filled in with compost (see fig. 16). With a little gentle tapping of the pot on the potting surface, and gentle pressure, the compost can be firmed into place.

After this, a thorough watering is essential. You may water from the top with a fine spray, again and again, until the water starts running out of the drainage holes. A sure way of saturating the whole soil-ball is to place the container in a bowl of water and submerge it. Two to four minutes will be sufficient. All air bubbles will rise to the top, and when they have ceased to appear, the ball will be thoroughly wet. However, the method of watering is immaterial—the important point is that the soil must be completely saturated. Do not jar or carry the container at this wet stage, as it will only pack the particles too close together, and this will take almost all the aeration out of the soil.

After transplanting, sunlight is not needed at all, as in most cases it can be fatal for the plant. The rule, after transplanting and root-pruning, is to keep the plant in the shade until it starts to produce fresh green buds. Then, given more and more sun, gradually, over a week or so, it can be moved back into full light.

THE THIRD AND SUBSEQUENT ROOT-PRUNING

The next root-pruning we do at the beginning of spring, that is, about eight months after the last root-pruning (the intermediate one).

The most favourable time to do this for the individual tree is when the buds of the new season have just formed and are about to burst. We take the tree, together with all the soil which is held by the root system (i.e. the root-ball), out of the container, cut off one-third of the volume from the base and the sides, and then turn the root-ball upside down and cut all the thicker roots further back still, as they will not have any future value; they can be reduced to as little as an inch in length, if you like.

These thick roots are not needed for the tree, and they will only be a hindrance when we finally transfer it to a shallow container. We can allow only the thicker roots which grow out of the trunk at the surface of the soil, or close to the surface, to remain, and these are cut back in such a way that their length is one-third less than the final length we need for the tree, determined by the shape and size of the final display container. These roots will later become exposed at the point where they leave the trunk. When replanting the tree in the container, we gently spread the roots out again so that they extend as naturally as possible towards the sides.

From then on we must root-prune the trees every spring in the same manner.

CHOICE OF FINAL CONTAINER

In most countries there are now various types of container available, and the size and shape is entirely up to you (see fig. 17). One word of warning: some containers have no drainage holes, or only a disc-shaped area where the material is thinner and can be easily knocked out. Others are completely glazed on the inside. Such containers are advertised as being suitable either for Ikebana flower arrangements, or for the planting

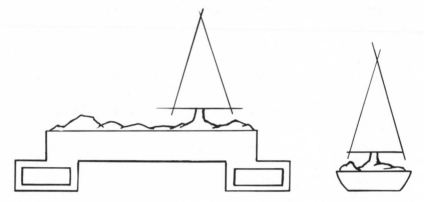

Fig. 17   The choice of the container is very important. If you want to emphasize the tree's perfection, and you do not mind the stiff and formal appearance, the right-hand example will serve the purpose. The container on the left, on the other hand, gives added space and an effect of landscape. The tree's appearance now suggests some dignity

of Bonsai trees and succulents, but in fact they should be avoided. If they are, however, unglazed on the inside (albeit undrained also), it is possible to use them, since drainage holes can be knocked into the base.

As regards the general appearance of Bonsai containers, one can only say that a good deal remains to be done.

The more space there is between the actual container and the level it is placed on, the greater is the dwarfing effect. The length of the legs or feet is the decisive factor here. The higher the tree and container come into the space, the more convincing is the dwarf. In other words, the more space all round, the smaller the tree appears to be. Many ways, in many different styles, can be employed here, and it is for you to use your imagination.

So far, there has been little emphasis on colour, except for blue, among Bonsai containers yet, here also, there are many possibilities regarding variety, contrast and dramatic effect. The general tendency so far is not to draw the attention too much to the container, and dull tones have been given preference. This has always created a high degree of monotony when trees are displayed together, as occurs at exhibitions.

For the final container, we generally choose pottery or ceramic. Here also, good drainage holes are essential, and a rough surface on the inside is beneficial, because roots dislike a smooth polished surface. Hollowed stones or slightly curved tiles are used as well, although the shallower the container, the more attention must be paid to watering. Practically all available Bonsai containers are rather clumsy and monotonous. For the artist with ideas, there is still very much scope for original design in this field.

When displayed, the container should be put at such a height that the soil surface is on a level with the eyes. We should be able to see our miniature tree from the same angle as we see the big trees. It is then that they reveal their whole beauty.

TRANSFER INTO THE FINAL DISPLAY CONTAINER

When we are satisfied with the overall appearance of our tree, we can shift it into a proper Bonsai container. The tree should have reached the

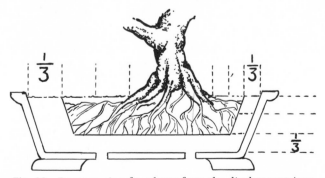

Fig. 18   Root-pruning for plants from the display container. The root-ball is reduced equally all round by one-third, measuring from the trunk to the wall of the container

stage at which we do not want vigorous growth any more. The transplanting is best done over two stages. The first root-pruning is as usual carried out in spring, but this time we cut off half the volume of the root-ball, and plant the tree in a tray not very much deeper than the root-ball.

Towards the last third of the growing season we again root-prune, this time to such an extent that the root-ball fits into the Bonsai container, and a layer of fresh compost can be placed on the base of the container. This layer need not be more than a quarter or a fifth of the total volume.

The following spring the routine root-pruning is carried out when the buds start to open, taking away one-third of the volume of root and soil, and leaving the remaining two-thirds undisturbed (see fig. 18). Before planting in the Bonsai container, we fill it one-third full with fresh compost, set the root-ball in position and fill in with compost, leaving a space at the top for watering.

5 · Principles of design and some variations

SHAPING

Formulating the design and shape of your tree will be much easier if you think of it as a structure composed of single lines (see figs. 4a–f, page 31).

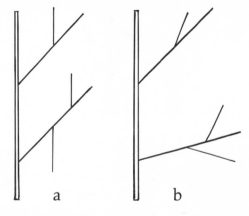

Fig. 19 Diagrammatic representation to show branches as single lines (a) symmetrical lines should be avoided (b) variations in angles indicate a more natural structure

For the actual sculpturing we must use these lines to the best advantage. Here are some basic rules valid for all shapes:

1. Decrease the distances between forking points gradually, the farther you are away from the trunk.
2. Avoid long straight lines, and rather change the direction as often as possible.
3. Do not have any crossing lines in the lower part of the tree. It is only in the higher part of the top that crossed lines will not irritate the eye of the viewer, and even then only a certain amount should be allowed.
4. Use foliage sparsely and let the framework be the dominant feature.
5. Do not hide the trunk and main branches with other branches which

start too low at the front. Only at the back can a lower branch be complementary to the skeleton of lines.

6. The eye will interpret any symmetry of lines as artificial and unnatural, and it is therefore to be avoided. Remember, you want to create the image of a tree, simply by putting lines of varying lengths together to form a single composition (see figs. 19–21). Your tree should look like a tree, even without any leaves. Keep it in the growing container until you have established a structure up to the seventh degree (see figs. 28–32, pages 94–8).

Fig. 20 (left) What to avoid: three lines coming from one point; laterals at a right angle; two laterals starting from the same level. (right) This model shows more natural shaping

Fig. 21 (left) Avoid: two laterals at the same angle; main branches on lower front of trunk; two laterals starting at one point. (right) A better solution

7. Old trees tend to have the overall lines rather drooping, while on young trees branches even thicker than on old specimens will still be pointing upwards. Over the years, heavy foliage and burdens of fruit, rain and snow will train the branches to a more or less gentle swoop downwards. Here we have to help our little trees, because the branches are too short to let this kind of ageing happen naturally.

The simplest way to do this is to supply this weighting ourselves. Lead weights as used for fishing are ideal. We fasten the necessary quantity of weights to one end of a piece of wire, bend the other end into a hook, and hang it on the branch in the most effective position. We are free to increase the effect of the weight at any time by moving the weights farther towards the end of the branch, or by slipping more weights on to the wire.

For training into any other than a downward position, I recommend the use of raffia; all ties round the trunk or a branch should be made loosely, so as not to cut into the bark. This will allow some space for thickening. The ideal time for tying-in is when the wood has just hardened and ripened, but only just. Green shoots tend to break when bent too hard.

8. On most species young shoots tend to grow straight upwards (see fig. 22). Here some action on our part is needed as well. To avoid a stiff formation like a broom, where all lines point up in the same direction, we have to open up the total structure, and incorporate some movement in the flow of branches. Wedges are a simple and most effective way of

Fig. 22 Young shoots growing straight upward, producing a formation like a broom

Fig. 23   Shoots can, however, be encouraged to grow downwards in a natural manner by using lead weights and wires formed into double-hook separators

spreading out the fan-like form of the lines. We bend wires (see fig. 23), and spread the lines to the required degree of opening, with the double-hook separators shown in the picture. To increase the variation, weights could be used at the same time on some of the straight ends.

The time it takes for such training varies with the species, the age and the thickness of the branch. In any case, the raffia or the weight have to be left in place for one growing season, from spring until autumn.

For improvement and correction, repeat the training in the next year, but never leave wire or raffia in place for two years in succession. To prevent marks appearing on the bark, it is better to take off the training material and use fresh every year.

PLANTING ON A STONE

A tree planted on top of a stone is more effective than one growing directly in the soil, because it brings the plant higher still above the soil, and thus gives it more space all round (see also plate 5). Such a presentation displays more of the structure in the upper part, and the greatly exposed root system helps the dramatic effect (see fig. 24a).

It is worthwhile training some species in this style, for the technique is as simple as for all the others. One has only to remember that the hardened roots may be exposed; the process in itself should proceed gradually and only when there are ample capillary roots lower down to feed the plant.

The ideal time to start training over a stone is when the seedling is still small. Pick a stone to fit your image of the final arrangement, that is, a stone big enough to support the size of the tree you have in mind. Place the seedling with the pruned roots on top in the required position. Try to make use of natural furrows into which you can direct the roots (see fig. 24b). Plant the two together in a growing container and fill in with soil so that the seedling is at the same depth as it was before transplanting.

The root-pruning at this stage will vary in comparison to the other styles. The amount of soil in the final container, underneath the stone, is the guide to the degree of root-pruning. If, for instance, the layer of soil under the stone in the final container is to be 2 inches, you would cut away two-thirds of an inch—that is, at every root-pruning, you remove one-third of the volume of soil beneath the stone (see fig. 24c). Apart from this, however, the annual root-pruning is done in exactly the same way as the intermediate one. A rearranging of roots can still be done at the intermediate root-pruning.

After two years, when doing the root-pruning, the plant and the stone are repotted a little higher than before, but the soil is still heaped up to cover all the roots. Watering will gradually wash away the surplus soil, and expose the roots around the trunk. In the following year, the stone can again be positioned higher, and more of the root system will become visible. As a general guide, I would recommend lifting the stone by about 1 inch a year, until you have reached the final position.

a

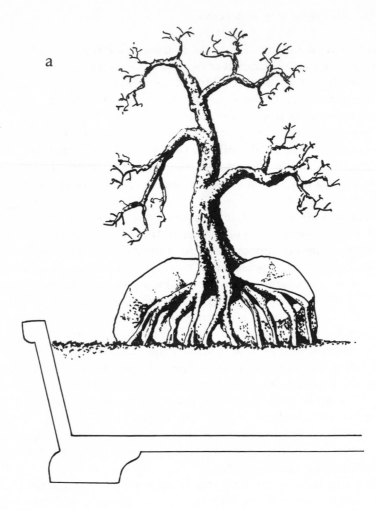

Fig. 24 Planting on a stone (a) *above* The fully formed tree with a greatly exposed root system spread over a stone (b) *top right* A seedling with the roots stopped, planted directly on top of a stone. The soil level for the seedling is kept as it was when the seedling was in the seed bed (c) *bottom right* The seedling on the stone after some time in the growing container. The criterion for the amount of root-pruning is the depth of the final display container

74

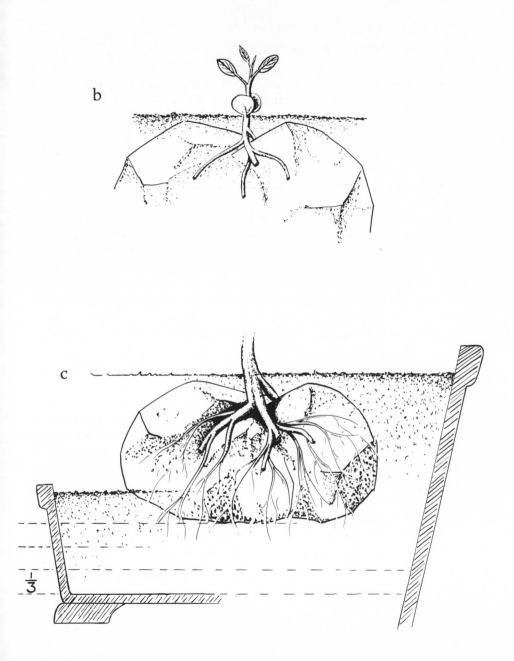

b

c

$\dfrac{1}{3}$

75

THE ONE-TRUNKED FOREST

A very rewarding style is the forest formed from one trunk, in which the main branches are used as trunks for individual trees. The trunk is planted horizontally, and so are the main branches up to the position of the individual tree. From there on the main branches are grown vertically, and used as trunks. The shaping of all the individual trees is done exactly as you would do with a single one (see fig. 25a).

The number of trees making the forest is up to you, although it will be an advantage if you choose an uneven number to avoid all symmetry.

For a start, the seedling is root-pruned at an early stage, in the same way that it is for other trees. Then, in a growing container, we let the plant develop the number of leaves we need for a corresponding quantity of single trees, and then stop it just above the bud in the position required for the highest main branch. After this, training in the horizontal line can begin when the stem above the soil starts to harden and has changed to a darker colour; the part where the bending has to be done should no longer be green. You may either tie the seedling in the desired position, or use the weight of a board to apply pressure gradually (see fig. 25b). The board can be pushed further along the trunk as the seedling grows (see fig. 25c).

When the new shoots appear, after the stopping of the seedling, remove the board and use laths instead, placing them at intervals to allow full light to reach the buds (see fig. 25d). The single shoots are grown horizontally, up to the point where the trunk of the individual tree is to be positioned. When a shoot has reached this point, training it into a vertical line can be started.

Do remember that the tip of a plant is the most vigorous part, and the tallest tree in your arrangement is best selected from shoots at the end of the horizontal trunk and never from a shoot close to the root system.

The placing of the individual trees is very important—do think it over

Fig. 25 (*opposite*) Training of a one-trunked forest (a) a layout for a one-trunked forest with nine individual trees (b) for a one-trunked forest, the seedling is trained horizontally either by tying or by using a board (c) the board is moved along as the seedling grows on (d) a one-trunked forest, in which seven main branches are being vertically trained to become individual trunks. The leaves have been omitted for clarity

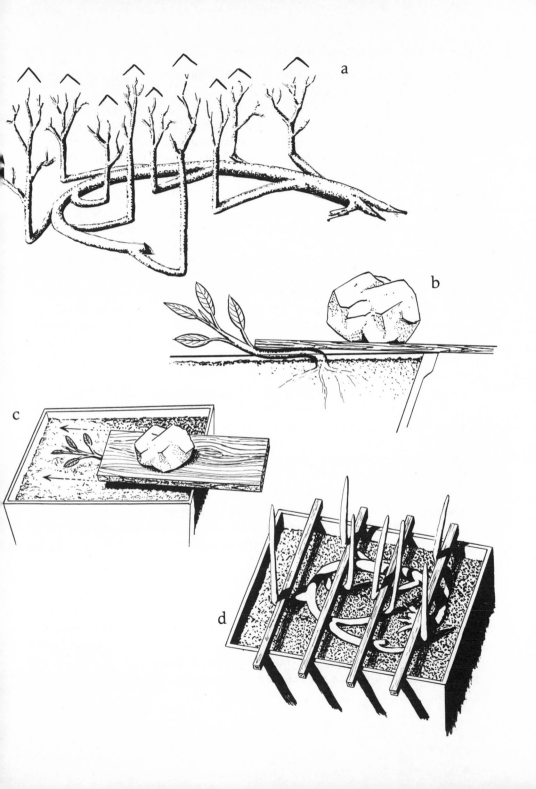

a

b

c

d

before you start. An oval or circular shape formed by the trunk might be the answer for a well spaced layout.

The single shoots, now trained into trunks, have to be fixed in their vertical position and must be held there for at least two years. If you are using raffia or wire, keep the loops slightly loose, to make sure the little trunks have space to thicken. The wire must never cut into the wood.

Each tree in the group is shaped as are single trees. Try to obtain as much variety as possible. Start with the lowest main branch at a different height on each tree, and ensure that the lines are at varying angles. Never have all the trees at the same height, and do not place the tallest tree in the centre.

The second root-pruning, which is the first in the growing container, is done at the beginning of the last third of the first growing season, and is the intermediate one. We reduce the volume of roots by one-third, leaving all the soil round the remaining two-thirds, and plant the shrunken root-ball back in the growing container. The missing third is filled up with fresh potting mixture. Every following root-pruning is always done in the early spring, when the new buds of the season have formed, but are not yet open.

When you are happy with the overall appearance of the forest, it is time to shift the arrangement to a display container, the final one. The routine is the same as for all other trees.

SHAPING OF OLD WOOD FROM NURSERY STOCK

When converting older plants to Bonsai, you have to take into consideration the fact that old wood is reluctant to produce new shoots. For this reason it is advisable to select material with a sufficient number of branches already coming from the trunk. At the top of a plant, it is always easy to improve the shape, but it is very nearly impossible to encourage new growth to come from the lower part of the trunk.

For the first step, remove all the soil round the trunk until you get down to the first strong roots. Then, with the full structure of the plant thus revealed, the main branches can be selected, and the unwanted ones cut off. After this, shape every main branch by eliminating the unwanted and unsightly laterals (see 'What makes a tree', p. 30). All long and straight lines are pruned back to a harmonious length.

Plate 9   *Acacia giraffea* (12″, 4½ years)

Then we remove the plant from the nursery container and cut the roots back by one-third all round, in the usual way. If it has only a long and stringy root formation, take off one-third of the volume from the bottom. Retain as much old soil as possible on the remaining two-thirds, and disturb the roots in this part as little as possible.

Then we plant the tree in a growing container (see 'The growing container', p. 48), the best time for doing this being the spring. When new green starts to appear on the plant, it is time to do any adjustments needed to the shape by using either weights, raffia or wire. All the new shoots are handled as explained in the section 'How to build up a tree', p. 49.

The next root-pruning is done the following spring, and every spring thereafter. The plant is transferred to a Bonsai container when the overall appearance is satisfactory to you, that is, when it looks the way you want it to look. Shifting from the growing container to the final display container is done in two stages, exactly as with trees grown from seedlings.

SHAPING OF OLD WOOD, PLANTS COLLECTED FROM THE WILD

I do not think there are any places left on our globe to which you can just go and pick a plant, unless you have the permission of the owner of the property first. Before you start, be well prepared to carry a big and heavy clump of soil, and the necessary tools, with you.

Since you want small, stunted plants with a height of under 2 feet (60 cm) you need only start digging in a circle about 2 feet away from the trunk. It is essential to find and retain as much of the root system as there is around the trunk. You should leave, as a minimum, the same volume of soil as the overall size of the tree. Long and unwanted shoots at the end you may cut away on the spot. The same applies to roots which are longer than the total height of the plant.

Try to keep the soil round the roots and wrap it all in moist hessian which can then be covered with protective plastic material, while it is being transported. Take some surplus soil from the spot for addition to the soil mixture in the growing container.

On return set the plant into a growing container, using half your

Plate 10   *Adansonia digitata*, Baobab (10", 5 years). Note the dwarfed leaves on the tree and the normal leaf on the right

potting mixture mixed with half the soil collected at the location of the plant. Pass it through a sieve and mix it well. The growing container should be big enough to take a layer of 4 inches (10 cm) of compost on the bottom beneath and round the root-ball. After thorough watering, do the main trimming as for plants from nursery stock, and when new green has appeared, start the training of bending and twisting. The next root-pruning is in early spring (see 'The growing container', p. 48). The ensuing steps are the same as for plants from seedlings.

In both cases, nursery plants or wild plants, you are faced with a structure on which you have had no influence so far. The main branches will seldom be in a favourable position, and the general flow of lines will look rather untidy and irritating. It is up to you to bring some harmony and grace to the structure, and hard pruning is the only way.

Bring the whole framework back to a certain degree of simplicity. Let only the clear and truly wanted lines stand. Save more of the branch formation on the lower part, and clear away more of the mass on top. The most difficult part of the whole operation is not only the selection of lines from a given structure, but also the building up of new elements. You will need patience, for plants which have grown under stunting conditions are slow in producing new material.

6 · Routine care and cultivation

WATERING

The most important rule here is: *never* let the soil become bone-dry.

Whenever you water the trees do it thoroughly. It will last longer, and the whole root system will benefit from it, not just the roots at the top. Every time, make sure the whole of the soil is saturated. The next watering will be as soon as you see signs of drying out on the soil surface. Remember, this can happen after only one hour, to a thimbleful of soil, or it may occur only every other day, if the container is the size of a bucket. In the resting season the trees will require much less water; during the growing season they will need more, and smaller containers will dry out faster than bigger ones. You have to learn by experience from the signs your own plants give you. Let me repeat: never let the soil become bone-dry.

SOIL

Besides being a support for the plant, the soil in our containers has other functions as well. An ideal mixture allows good drainage for the surplus water, but holds a certain amount of moisture at the same time. It should not be packed too tight, but rather should have some aeration between the particles. A mixture with such qualities would have a high percentage of granular substance in it, but only a small quantity of clay. A mixture of granular soil and sand only does not retain the moisture very well, but used in a compost with a suitable proportion of peat or similar material, it can help to give the necessary drainage.

For a general guide, I recommend a mixture as follows: two-thirds of sandy material, in which the sand should be less coarse than river sand;

Plate 11   *Tecoma* (12", 4 years)

84

one-third of moisture-retaining material, which can be a compost of peat, clay and vermiculite mixed together in equal parts. The potting mixture will therefore consist of one-third of the compost and two-thirds of sandy material without any extra ingredient such as clay and so on. This mixture will provide good drainage and still retain the essential moisture.

If clay only was used for water retention, the mixture would become too sticky, and would not have enough aeration. If, on the other hand, vermiculite and peat were used as the only water absorbing ingredients, it would be necessary to feed right from the beginning, since neither substance has any nutrients suitable for the plant, and they are used only for their ability to hold moisture.

FERTILISER

The nourishment present in the soil is not the only food that a plant needs and absorbs. Oxygen and carbon dioxide, taken from the atmosphere, are also essential for healthy growth. Another necessity is light or, to be more precise, sunlight. With the help of light as energy, soluble minerals are transformed into nourishing substances. This process—photosynthesis—takes part in the leaves. Plants ingest through the semi-permeable walls of their cells, and this allows for absorption only of diluted substances. It is important to remember that your tree can make use of the fertiliser you add only when there is a certain degree of moisture in the soil.

The three main elements needed by plants are nitrogen, phosphorus and potassium, although there are quite a number of other elements which either have their own effective characteristics or act chemically in union with others. We refer to them as 'trace' elements, because they are needed by the plant in small quantities only.

Here are some of the more important of these: calcium, magnesium, sulphur, manganese, iron, boron, chlorine and sodium. You need not specialise in single fertilisers for different species of trees.

However, it is necessary to give your plants the three basic elements, plus the trace elements. All over the world we now give fertiliser either in the powder form of dry mineral salts or as liquids. For the grower of pot plants, most dealers offer mixtures based on average plant demands

Plate 12 *Erythrina lysistemon*, Kaffirboom (9½″, 4 years)

with trace elements added. Before you buy one or another, read the label and make sure there are trace elements in it.

Let me give you one word of warning—use the fertiliser exactly as advised by the manufacturer. Never use a stronger dose, and if you vary the instructions at all, use less than recommended. It is better still to use natural enrichment, such as compost, and add fertiliser only as a supplement, just to make sure all that is needed will be present in your potting compost.

TROUBLES

The weak and unhealthy plants are the ones which are first attacked by pests. If you give your trees all they need to keep them healthy, they will be less susceptible to pests and diseases. Give the plants ample light, and never let the soil dry out completely. Keep the soil in good heart, to provide all the necessary nourishment. Make it a routine to have a good look at all your trees at regular intervals.

Aphids (greenfly), scale insect and red spider mite are the most common pests, and mildew the most troublesome fungus disease; it takes the form of a white powdery coating on leaves and stems. However, it is best to consult your favourite gardening store for a remedy. It is impossible to recommend any particular insecticide here since proprietary names for the various chemicals change from country to country. Take a sample from the sick tree along to the nurseryman, if you are not sure about the pest or disease you have detected on the plant. He will give you advice on what to use and which will be the most economical treatment, i.e. dusting powder or a liquid spray.

Whenever you notice any trouble, do not delay but take action at once. All pests and diseases are fought much more easily in the early stages.

TOOLS

In every hobby or craft, one can employ a great range of highly specialised tools, yet it is possible in this case to do very well with a limited set, at least for the start. I have listed here only the ones which you will really need, the essentials:

1. Set of 3 cutting tools—a pair of strong secateurs, a pair of medium-size scissors, and very small scissors, similar to manicure scissors, for fine work
2. A sieve with a mesh of about $\frac{1}{16}$th inch in diameter
3. A watering-can or bottle—it can be a plastic bottle with holes burned or drilled in the top
4. Wire, single or double plastic-covered electric wire; raffia, and gauze, not metal but man-made fibre (nylon, etc.)

7 · Display and competitive exhibition

DISPLAY

There is one position only at which a miniature tree in a container is shown to the best advantage: that is when the eyes of the viewer are at a slightly higher level than the surface of the soil (see fig. 26). This will

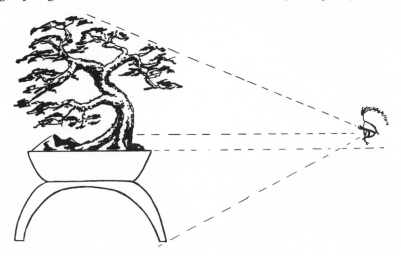

Fig. 26   The ideal point from which to look at a potted tree is when the eyes are slightly above the rim of the container

give the same impression as one would have if standing on the ground viewing a normal sized tree some yards away from it.

Any object is always observed in relation to the space around it. For our displays of miniature trees, this means we have to give them plenty of space. The ideal would be to have the container floating in space, but hanging it from wires does not, as one might think, solve the problem.

Display and competitive exhibition

It is better to use a single stand, pillar, pedestal, and so on, with just enough surface area to place the container on top of it. The ideal background will consist of one light colour. For public exhibitions, however, rows of such stands at one level, with a neutral coloured backdrop could be monotonous, and we must therefore try to introduce some variety.

Keeping in mind the closeness to eye level, we can dispose the trees on a longer table in a kind of terrace or step system of arrangement so that they are at varying heights. This will do much to break the uniform appearance. Brightly coloured areas, either for the standing surface or the backdrop, can help to change the mood, or dramatise a single display. One may go as far as to display a single tree on and in front of black velvet.

For the arrangements it is worthwhile remembering that the viewer need not come closer than double the height of the tree. A tree with a height of 1 foot should be seen from a distance of 2 feet, but in front of a tree with a height of 3 feet, the viewer must have space to observe from a distance of 6 feet. For exhibitions the source of light should be well above eye level. The most effective way of providing illumination is to give each tree its own individual light, as this indicates sunshine.

When displaying trees at home, we can take into consideration the fact that they are observed most of the time while we are sitting down. This brings the level of display down in comparison with the public exhibition at which people look while walking or standing. Avoid all distracting objects in the vicinity of a displayed tree, and your visitors will be constantly attracted by the lines and the shape, perhaps because it is a living thing, perhaps because of its own personal aura.

STYLES

We have had a preliminary look at shapes (see p. 32) in order to become familiar with natural growing habits and their variations. For judging and identification, potted trees are classified into definite styles:

ONE-TRUNKED   upright (fig. 27a)
                       slanting (fig. 27b)
                       semi-cascading (fig. 27c)
                       cascading (fig. 27d)

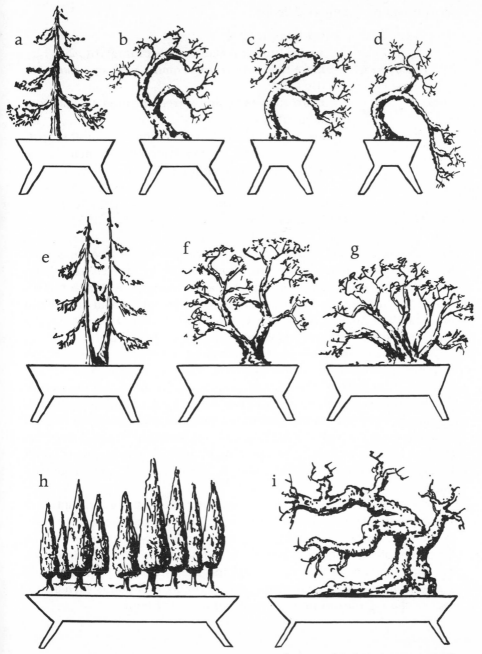

Fig. 27   Styles of tree. Top row, left to right: one-trunked upright, slanting, semi-cascading, cascading. Centre row: two-trunked upright, varied, and multi-trunked. Bottom row, more than two single trees on one container, and an artistic arrangement

TWO-TRUNKED	upright (fig. 27e)
	varied (upright, slanting, cascading) (fig. 27f)
MULTI-TRUNKED	more than two trunks coming from one rootstock (fig. 27g)
FOREST	more than two single trees planted in one container (fig. 27h)
ORNAMENTAL	all trees which bear no relation to natural shapes, and where the overall impression is more of an artistic arrangement (fig. 27i)

JUDGING POTTED TREES

The following system is based on merit, and it is meant as a suggestion for clubs and societies sponsoring shows. It can be applied anywhere, regardless of local conditions, without being changed. A Bonsai society which has just been formed, or a circle of people with an advanced and high standard can equally well make use of the system. How they apply it depends on how far they have advanced with their skills.

The flexible approach is recommended wherever beginners get together for their first competitions. To avoid disappointment for the majority of beginners, the basis of judging could simply be the overall number of trees sent in by an exhibitor for each class in the competition. Gradually, over the years, a committee could raise the standard of local competition by taking as a judging base the standard of the district or, later, of the entire country. For even more difficult events, points could be given according to world-wide standards to raise and encourage quality.

Since the tree is the centre piece of our interest I have allotted a maximum of 20 points in four different groups, for the appearance only, of the tree. Then there are three groups, each of which can provide a maximum of 5 points, as a reward for presentation and artistic effort. To encourage an interest in variety and the wider use of indigenous species, I have added two groups of a maximum of 5 points each again, each of these groups supplying points as a kind of bonus.

	Max. no of points
Overall appearance as a tree	20
Degree of harmony between all parts of the framework (trunk, branches, twigs)	20
Degree of leaf dwarfing	20
Degree of artistry achieved between lines and spacing	20

Supplementary points

The degree of harmony between the container and the tree, or the effect of the container as a complementary or dramatising attribute	5
Natural or artistic handling of the underplanting and landscaping	5
Handling of the root formation (exposed roots, roots clasping a stone, etc.)	5

Bonus points

An indigenous species	5
Every 'First' of a species in club, district, city, country or the world	5

A grouping similar to the following 5 groups would make it possible to have competitions within each of them, For example, a young tree competing in the class for 'Prospective Material' could find a place there, and work its way up into the next class of 'Promising Trees', without competing right from the beginning against the top class trees such as the 'Exhibition Trees' or the 'Perfection' class.

	Points
Class 1: Perfection	80–105
Class 2: Exhibition trees	60–80
Class 3: Promising trees	40–60
Class 4: Prospective material	20–40
Class 5: Starting and training specimens	under 20

DIAGRAMMATIC REPRESENTATIONS TO SHOW STAGES OF BUILD-UP DEPENDING ON TYPE OF GROWTH AND DESIGN REQUIRED

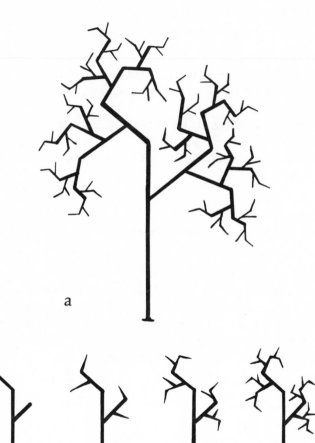

Fig. 28 (a) a structure using the alternate form of build-up (b) the progressive stages to the final tree, when using alternate shoots

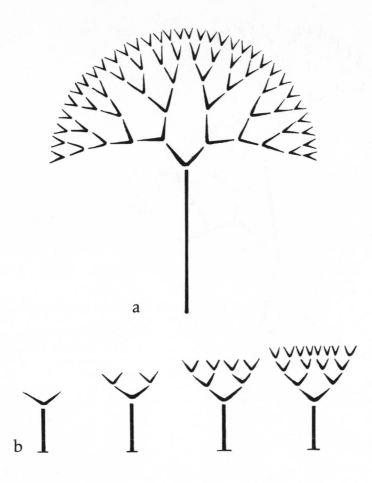

a

b

Fig. 29 (a) a structure using the simple fork at every stage (b) the single phases for continuous forking build-up to the stage shown at (a)

a

Fig. 30 (a) three main branches are developed in one stage, and then the forked system is applied (b) the progressive stages for this development, with the trunk and main branches, first, second and third degree laterals produced in succession

b

a

Fig. 31 (a) example of a structure formed by one shoot and one leader (b) the trunk and the first main branch, together with the leader (c) the second main branch and the leader. Laterals of the first degree appear on the first main branch (d) the third main branch and the leader, plus laterals of the second degree on the first main branch, and the laterals of the first degree on the second main branch (e) the fourth main branch plus the leader. There are now third degree laterals on the first main branch, second degree laterals on the second main branch, and first degree laterals on the third main branch

b

c

d

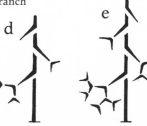

e

97

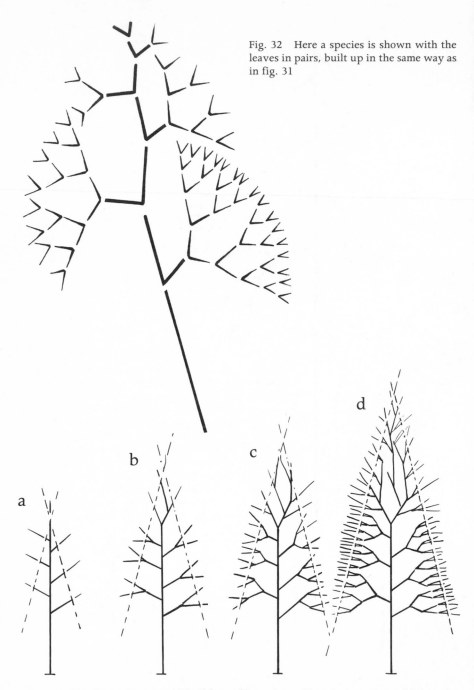

Fig. 32 Here a species is shown with the leaves in pairs, built up in the same way as in fig. 31

Fig. 33 Simultaneous pyramid build-up of branches (a) main branches (b) laterals, 1st degree (c) laterals, 2nd degree (d) laterals, 3rd degree

Appendix · Comparison table

THE NEW TECHNIQUE   THE TRADITIONAL TECHNIQUE

Training—first step (roots)

Starts with a very young seed-ling in the first year, when the first true leaves (two or three) have developed, about four to eight weeks after germination. At this stage seedlings of most species still have four to eight capillary roots, besides the tap root.

Starts only in the second or third year after germination. The thickened stem (future trunk) is the primary aim, as in the early beginning, when only plants dug out of the ground were used.

Action—1

Remove the growing tips from all the root ends.

Prune the thick roots round the stem to fit the Bonsai container.

Reaction

Densified root system round the future trunk, right from the beginning.

Thick roots are slow to produce new capillary roots.

Action—2

Plant in growing container. Use as much soil as possible, the minimum being the total volume of the visualised tree:

Plant in Bonsai container. Use small amount of soil only.

THE NEW TECHNIQUE	THE TRADITIONAL TECHNIQUE
Reaction	
Unlimited nourishment (due to unlimited root system), normal growth rate, and even growth all over.	Limited nourishment (due to limited root system), slow growth, and uneven and small growth.

Training—second step (branches)

The main growing point of the seedling is stopped when it has either the right number of leaves, or leaves at the desired positions, depending on the number and position of laterals wanted.	New side shoots are stopped in the second half of the growing season. That is, in the third or fourth year after germination for the very first time.

Reaction

New shoots, the first laterals, are produced. These will be the main branches appearing from the remaining leaf-axils. Shoots pointing in the wrong direction or appearing at unwanted positions, are removed at the bud stage.	The leaves of this following (secondary) growth are smaller than the previous ones.

Training—third and further steps

Newly developed shoots are
stopped (the second stopping)
as soon as they have reached the
desired stage, i.e. when they
have the required number of
leaves, or leaves in the positions
wanted.

THE NEW TECHNIQUE   THE TRADITIONAL TECHNIQUE

Reaction

Secondary growth is smaller   Dwarfed leaves appear only and
than the previous one. This   truly after the previous stop-
effect increases with every   ping, towards the end of a
further stopping in succession   season. This applies as well for
during one season.   old and established trees of
                                     world fame.

Root-pruning

First, at the stage of a young   Once in every spring.
seedling.
Second, at the beginning of the
second half of the first growing
season.
Third, at the beginning of the
second growing season.
Fourth and further, every
spring.

Reaction on deciduous trees

When trained in this way, the   The first new leaves of a new
first new leaves of a new season   season are as big as the normal
are as small as the last ones of   size leaves. No true dwarfing
the previous season.   effect. Consequently no big-
                                     leaved species can be used, let
                                     alone any of the giant-leaved
                                     ones.

Dwarfing of foliage

Less than $\frac{1}{100}$th of its original   Not less than $\frac{1}{10}$th of its original
size.   size.

Speed of dwarfing

For large-leaved species, within   For species with small or

THE NEW TECHNIQUE	THE TRADITIONAL TECHNIQUE
four years after germination. A height of 1 foot only is needed even for large-leaved species, to bring all the features—foliage and structure—into harmony with each other.	medium size leaves, twenty to fifty years. Species with normal or medium size leaves have to be brought up to a height of 3 feet and more, to achieve a certain degree of harmony and relation between foliage and structure.

Basic differences

Growing process

Everything is planned right from the beginning—the entire finished structure of a tree, with all its characteristics, number and places of main branches, and stage of laterals in various degrees, is envisaged from the start.	Everything has to be left to chance. The system does not guarantee a definite reaction of a particular kind to the training undertaken at each stage.

Sculpturing

The creating of a miniature tree follows the natural production of growth, building up progressively from the trunk, with main branches and laterals as they appear. All units can be directed towards the final target. The tree is sculptured from bottom to top, one unit after the other, and shaped at the same time. Exact positioning is possible through free choice of selection in number and places of all branches.	Planning is limited and thus, also, free creation. The grower has to convert existing material into harmonious shapes and the required appearance. He is left with little choice as far as the selection and placing of all branches is concerned. The final structure is always a compromise, a concession to the existing structure which was the basis for the start.

THE NEW TECHNIQUE	THE TRADITIONAL TECHNIQUE
The tree is built up in a natural rhythm of succession, starting with the trunk and proceeding with the main branches, branchlets, and so on; they thicken equally all over, like the normal tree.	The difference in thickness between the trunk and branches can only be overcome in decades.
The new technique is based on the fact that a dwarf leaf can be established without any root limitation or pruning. Furthermore, this dwarfing is effective higher up the tree, and takes place more rapidly, and all species respond to it.	The traditional technique is based on the fact that limited nourishment produces small growth. In reality, the technique recommends one to copy nature where nature is imperfect.
A tree trained to be a miniature structure before reaching maturity adopts these dwarf characteristics faster, and retains them permanently.	It is not only difficult but time consuming as well, to impose dwarfing characteristics on older plants.

In a nutshell

Involves dwarfing through growing. It is applicable to all species.	Consists of dwarfing through stunting. It is only effective on small-leaved species.

Index

Index

red spider mite, 87
replanting, 64–5, 67–8, 80
roots, growth characteristics, 37, 38–40
   planting on stones, 73–5
   pruning, 23, 39–40, 59–64, 65, 73, 76,
     78, 80, 99–100, 101

scale insect, 87
Schizolobium excelsum, Plate 2
seeds, germination, 38, 47–8
shapes, 32–5, 90–2, 94–8
shaping, 69–82
shoots, pruning, 21, 53–4, 58–9, 76
size, 24, 30
soil, 47, 49, 81–2, 83–5

spruce, 58
stones, planting on, 73–5

Tecoma, Plate 11
temperature, 19, 20, 47, 57
tools, 87–8
traditional techniques, 20–2, 99–103
transplanting, 64–5, 67–8, 80
Tridend maple, Plate 8

water and watering, 19, 43, 64–7, 73,
   82, 83
weighting, 70, 72, 76
wild plants, 80–1